Arthur Crawshay Alliston Hall

The Gospel woes

Lent Sermons

Arthur Crawshay Alliston Hall

The Gospel woes
Lent Sermons

ISBN/EAN: 9783337116996

Printed in Europe, USA, Canada, Australia, Japan

Cover: Foto ©ninafisch / pixelio.de

More available books at **www.hansebooks.com**

THE GOSPEL WOES

Lent Sermons

BY

RT. REV. A. C. A. HALL, D.D.
BISHOP OF THE DIOCESE OF VERMONT

NEW YORK
JAMES POTT & CO., PUBLISHERS
114 FIFTH AVENUE
1896

COPYRIGHT, 1891, BY
JAMES POTT & CO.

TROW'S
PRINTING AND BOOKBINDING COMPANY,
NEW YORK.

PREFACE.

THESE Sermons were preached on the Sunday mornings in Lent, 1890, in the Mission Church of S. John the Evangelist, Boston. They have been subsequently written out for publication in the hope that they may suggest helpful thoughts for meditation on one aspect of our Lord's teaching, an aspect to which our time would seem to give less than its due prominence. With the exception of S. Matthew xxiv. 19, all the Woes pronounced by our Lord, as recorded by the different Evangelists, are considered in these Sermons. In them, as in other publications, the author is much more largely indebted to others' thoughts than he has often been able to acknowledge.

MISSION HOUSE OF S. JOHN EVANGELIST, BOSTON.
EPIPHANY, 1891.

CONTENTS.

		PAGE
I.	THE WOE ON WORLDLY EASE AND CONTENTMENT	7
II.	THE WOE ON WORLDLY POPULARITY	21
III.	THE WOE ON THE ABUSE OF RELIGIOUS PRIVILEGES	36
IV.	THE WOE ON OFFENCES	49
V.	THE WOE ON HYPOCRISY	67
VI.	THE WOE ON THE TRAITOR	82

I.

THE WOE ON WORLDLY EASE AND CONTENTMENT.

"Woe unto you that are rich! for ye have received your consolation.
Woe unto you that are full! for ye shall hunger.
Woe unto you that laugh now! for ye shall mourn and weep."—S. LUKE vi. 24, 25.

WE are to consider on the Sunday mornings in this Lent the Gospel Woes. You will understand that it is not in the way of gloomy denunciation or critical thought of others that we are to regard them, but so that we may avoid their falling on ourselves.

In this spirit we will consider the Woe pronounced by Jesus Christ our Lord in the Gospel

(1) On Worldly Ease and Contentment, as in the text;

(2) On Worldly Popularity—"Woe unto you when all men speak well of you;"[1]

---

[1] S. Luke vi. 26.

(3) On the Abuse of Religious Privileges—"Woe unto you Chorazin and Bethsaida;"[1]

(4) On those who put Stumbling-blocks in the way of others—"It must be that offences come, but woe to that man by whom the offence cometh;"[2]

(5) On Hypocrisy, such as was illustrated in the conduct of the Scribes and Pharisees.[3]

(6) On the Traitor—"Woe unto him by whom the Son of Man is betrayed."[4]

In thinking Whose these several utterances were, one is reminded of Dr. Newman's touching and most thoughtful lines concerning the severity of Christian teaching with regard to the consequence or punishment of evil and "The Wrath to Come:"

> "Christ on Himself, considerate Master, took
> The utterance of that doctrine's fearful sound.
> The Fount of Love His servants sends to tell
> Love's deeds; Himself reveals the sinner's Hell."[5]

From a lower point of view, looking at our Lord's Human life, we may helpfully ask, *Who* spake the words of Woe that we are specially to consider to-day?

"Woe unto you that are rich! for ye have your consolation.

---

[1] S. Matt. xi. 20–24.　　[2] S. Matt. xviii. 7.
[3] S. Matt. xxiii. 23–28.　　[4] S. Matt. xxvi. 24.
[5] *Lyra Apostolica*, lxxxiii.

Woe unto you that are full! for ye shall hunger.
Woe unto you that laugh now! for ye shall mourn and weep."

It is the utterance of no cynical pessimist, disparaging earthly life in proud discontent, and careless and indifferent to others' interests, their joys or sorrows. He Who spake thus had fed the fainting multitude, and provided wine to cheer the wedding-feast at Cana. He would have His disciples rejoice with them that rejoiced, as well as weep with them that wept.

Nor was this the envious utterance of a social revolutionist working for a general upheaval of the established order, in which the prosperous might be dragged down and the needy climb up on their ruin. He Who so spake had voluntarily renounced for Himself that against which He warns others. Though He was rich, yet for our sakes He became poor, that we through His poverty might be made truly rich.[1] He is Himself the Man of Sorrows, and He promises blessings, a counterpart of these Woes, on the poor, on those that hunger and that mourn. Whatever the form of words the tone is of pity rather than of denunciation; the utterance is not an imprecation, but a solemn warning not unmixed with sympathy.

---

[1] 2 Cor. viii. 9.

The key to our Lord's meaning is to be found in the explanatory clause appended to the first Woe. "Woe unto you that are rich! *for ye have your consolation.*" The verb is the same that our Lord uses when He warns against the performing of religious exercises, prayer, fasting, almsgiving, with a view to being seen of men. Those who so act, He says, "*have* their reward;" have it, that is, in full measure.[1] They have what they sought. They work for human applause, and they receive it. They are paid in full. So here. "Ye have all your consolation—all that you have a care for, all therefore that you can have."

I. On this we may well pause to note the general law of God's dealing with men. In the moral no less than in the material universe the law of Retribution prevails. God gives to all what they really seek. Set yourself really to work for an end, and you may gain it, whatever it is worth. You may gain pleasure, money, position. The folly of sin is not so much that men miss what they aim at, as that they miss a true aim; they set before them a mistaken aim. They get what they seek for, and when they have it, lo, it is not

---

[1] S. Matt. vi. 2, 5, 16.

what they expected. God gives them their desire, and sends leanness withal into their soul.[1] This is the truth expressed by S. Paul in figurative language concerning the Moral Harvest. "Be not deceived; God is not mocked: for whatsoever a man soweth, that shall he also reap. For he that soweth to his flesh shall of the flesh reap corruption; but he that soweth to the spirit shall of the spirit reap life everlasting."[2]

Two kinds of life, both seeking after good, each sowing its own seed and each reaping its appropriate harvest, are contrasted as "sowing to the flesh" and "sowing to the spirit." We are not to limit the former to gross and sensual living. The two stand for what are elsewhere called the Natural and the Spiritual or Regenerate life, a walking by faith and a walking by sight. Every man understands more or less the difference between the two—the goods sought by the one and by the other life. It is the difference between prosperity and well-doing, between indulgence and nobleness, between comfort and inward peace, between pleasure and striving after perfection, between happiness and blessedness.[3]

---

[1] Ps. cvi. 15.   [2] Gal. vi. 7, 8.
[3] *The Principle of the Spiritual Harvest*, in Fredk. Wm. Robertson's Sermons (1st Series).

Men labor for one or for the other; and in great measure they gain what they work for. Aims bounded by the horizon of this world reap wealth, reputation, position, comfort. But what is this but a harvest of corruption, poor blighted ears of useless grain which only mock those who spend their money for that which is not bread, their labor for that which satisfieth not? Luxuriance there may be in the harvest, but real rottenness.

Here I should like to read a most admirable letter (which some may have seen in the public prints) written by Dr. Lyman Abbott to the editor of a Southern newspaper, who put to him certain questions about the Christian religion, the answers to which were to be published in his paper:

"Belief in Jesus Christ is not an easy method of gaining happiness and life eternal. Salvation is not a crown, a robe, a harp, and a palace. Character is salvation, and there is no short and easy way to it. The heresy of heresies—worst of all heresies, labelled or unlabelled, that have ever corrupted mankind—is the notion that there is some way by which a man may get admission into heaven without purity, truth, love. Heaven is purity, truth, love. No man can get into heaven unless heaven gets into him. The blessedness of heaven is to be poor in spirit, meek, merciful, pure in heart. The kingdom of God is not meat and drink, nor songs and golden streets, but righteousness and peace and joy in the Holy Ghost—that is, in the fellowship of Him who is Himself Righteousness and Peace and Joy. Believing in the Lord Jesus Christ is not a substitute for obedience, but a method and a standard of obedience. We believe in Him when we obey Him.

"Why do not large numbers of persons avail themselves of His offer? For the simple reason that it has no attractions to them. They do not believe that to be poor in spirit, to be meek, to be merciful, to be pure in heart, is to be blessed. Their beatitudes—the beatitudes they really believe in—are of a different order; they read as follows:

"Blessed are the high-spirited: for theirs is the kingdom of the earth."

"Blessed are the grasping: for they shall get possession of the earth."

"Blessed are they which do hunger and thirst after riches: for they shall be filled."

"Blessed are the proud: for they shall have their own way."

"Blessed are the pleasure-seekers: for they shall have a good time."

"To believe in Jesus Christ is to revolutionize these ideals; to care very little for conditions, and a great deal for character; to count it more blessed to give than to receive, to serve than to be served, to be than to have, to see God than to acquire the earth. Believing in Christ means thinking as Christ thought, estimating life as Christ estimated it, obeying Christ, following Christ, doing as Christ did, becoming Christ-like. This is very simple; but it is not easy. Large numbers of people do not avail themselves of Christ's offer because they do not really care for what Christ offers. They want to be happy, but they are not particularly desirous to be good. And it is goodness which Christ offers to those that believe in Him, obey Him, follow Him."

II. You see what it is on which Jesus our Lord pronounces this Woe. It is not riches, nor rich men, as such. It is the temper that rests in worldly prosperity, that finds in earthly things its consolation and satisfaction. The Woe is on Worldly Contentment and Ease. In the parable of the Rich Man and Lazarus,[1] which is a kind of illustration of this declaration of our Lord, Dives was not in torment because he was rich, but because he was selfish, and being rich spent all on himself; because while he was clothed in purple and fine linen, and fared sumptuously every day, he left

---

[1] S. Luke xvi. 19.

Lazarus uncared for at his gate; he failed to recognize the responsibility that attached to his position, the stewardship for the wealth that was entrusted to him. And Lazarus was not in Abraham's bosom simply because he was a beggar or poor, but because he was contented. Wealth rightly used does not shut out from Heaven. Nor does Poverty patiently borne admit thereto. You may sell your soul for a dollar as well as for a thousand. Avarice may be manifested in sanding sugar as in watering stocks. Judas betrayed his Master for thirty pieces of silver, the price of a slave. Certainly it is not the rich as such on whom Jesus pronounces woe any more than He pronounced the poor as such necessarily blessed. A Nicodemus and a Joseph of Arimathæa will be welcomed with open arms as readily as the poorest man in Israel.

III. These very names serve as an illustration that in part explains our Lord's Woe on Worldly Prosperity. They illustrate the evil and dangers of wealth, the way in which Worldly Prosperity may involve us in this Woe. Nicodemus and Joseph were both high in station, members of the Sanhedrin, the ruling body among the Jews. And both were kept back from avowing themselves disciples of Jesus through fear of losing social position.[1] Nicodemus comes by night to learn of Him. Joseph also is a disciple secretly for fear of the Jews. How often is their case repeated! Instead of wealth being used for its legitimate ends, it serves to hold people back. What would So and So say? is the question asked by those who would lead in society. Instead of ruling they are ruled, slaves to popular opinion. How hardly, with what difficulty, shall the rich enter into the kingdom of Heaven!"

IV. Prosperity, Social Position, Ease of Life, to which our Lord refers, against the peril of which He warns His hearers, has another danger. It directly tends to deaden spiritual susceptibilities. It kills our nobler ambitions. Wealth tends to clog the finer spiritual sensibilities of the soul, and you see men, as the Psalmist says, whose hearts are as fat as brawn,[3] literally so cased and padded in the things of this life as to have lost altogether their sense of the supernatural.

It was said by a great English economist, Mr. Richard Cobden, "Sir, when I go to church there is one prayer which I say with my whole soul. 'In all time of our wealth [so the petition runs in the English Litany],

---

[1] S. John iii. 2; vii. 50; xix. 38, 39.
[2] S. Matt. xix. 23. [3] Ps. cxix. 70.

Good Lord deliver us.'" Aye, and we have much reason to pray that prayer. Deliver us from the quiet selfishness; deliver us from the grosser temptations; but deliver us above all from the blinding, numbing, paralyzing power of easy circumstances, which make death and the great realities beyond it an unwelcome thought.[1] Worldly prosperity is so apt to become worldly ease and contentment. The temptation is so great to settle down and make our home here, in the spirit of the rich fool.[2]

It was for this reason that our Lord counselled the rich young man, in whom He saw such possibilities for good that looking on him He loved him, to go and sell all that he had, and to follow Him in poverty. Jesus saw that his great possessions were a hindrance to his perfection, held him back from a full and free surrender to Jesus as His disciple.[3]

We can understand now the remarkable difference between the Beatitudes as recorded by S. Matthew in the Sermon on the Mount, and those given by S. Luke in the Sermon on the Plain.[4] The discourses seem to be distinct, delivered on different occasions, and to somewhat different classes of hearers. S. Luke

---

[1] Dr. Liddon's Sermon on *Personal Responsibility for the Gift of Revelation.*
[2] S. Luke xii. 19. [3] S. Mark x. 21.
[4] S. Matt. v. 3–11; S. Luke vi. 20–22.

omits the qualifying moral condition which is given in S. Matthew, "Blessed are the poor *in spirit*, Blessed are they that hunger and thirst *after righteousness.*" Our Lord blesses the outward condition, of poverty and outward need, as a means to gaining the higher spiritual disposition. Outward poverty should tend to poverty of spirit; the absence of earthly satisfaction to hungering and thirsting after righteousness.

Lent, my brethren, is a time to lay these things to heart. We are bidden now more especially to commune with our own heart and in our chamber and be still; to break through the crust of material comfort, to abstain from earthly and social pleasures, to take account of ourselves and of our position before God, to weigh ourselves in the measures of the sanctuary. Certainly there is a real danger against which we have to guard in our time of advancing material civilization, that this be not detrimental to true progress, that the inner man be not drowned, as it were, and smothered, as is quite possible, by the very civilization that our hands have wrought. A man's life, we need continually to be reminded, consists not in the abundance of things which he possesseth.[1]

---

[1] S. Luke xii. 15.

A familiar Psalm expresses the truth:

> "While many are saying, 'O for the sight of good fortune!'
> Jehovah, lift Thou up the light of Thy face upon us [so the faithful pray].
> Thou hast put more joy into my heart
> Than when others have their corn and new wine in abundance."[1]

To Laodicea was sent the warning message: "Because thou sayest, I am rich and am increased in goods, and have need of nothing; and knowest not that thou art wretched and miserable and poor and blind and naked: I counsel thee to buy of me gold refined by fire that thou mayest be rich." . . .

"As many as I love I rebuke and chasten," adds the Lord.[2] "God in mercy mingles bitterness with earthly pleasures," says S. Chrysostom, "that we may seek another felicity whose sweetness does not deceive." I may conclude with a quotation from the Bampton Lectures of the Bishop of Ripon, Dr. Boyd Carpenter:

"If the end which is set before us be the education of our characters, then we shall not think it strange that we are called on to struggle, permitted to fall, given the experiences of

---

[1] Ps. iv. 6-8. (Cheyne's translation.)
[2] Rev. iii. 17-19.

success, and exposed to the vicissitudes and the seasonal trials of life,

> 'Esteeming sorrow, whose employ
> Is to develop, not destroy,
> Far better than a barren joy.'

For it is thus that a Divine Love deals with us, that in the end we may become possessed of that wealth which the world cannot take away, the spiritual wealth of a perfected and developed character." [1]

---

[1] *The Permanent Elements in Religion*, p. 323.

II.

THE WOE ON WORLDLY POPULARITY.

"Woe unto you when all men shall speak well of you! For so did their fathers to the false prophets."
—S. LUKE vi. 26.

THIS Woe on Worldly Popularity was pronounced by our Lord along with those which we considered last Sunday on Worldly Ease and Contentment. The others which we have set down for the remaining Sundays in Lent were all uttered on separate and distinct occasions.

These earlier Woes are peculiar to S. Luke, recorded by him alone.

"Woe unto you that are rich, for ye have received your consolation.

"Woe unto you that are full now, for ye shall hunger.

"Woe unto you that laugh now, for ye shall mourn and weep.

"Woe unto you when all men shall speak well of you."

It is as if S. Luke as a physician of the soul treasured up and recorded our Lord's warnings against the perilous temptations that worldly prosperity and success, of whatever kind, bring with them.

You will remember that these four Woes of S. Luke correspond with the four Blessings recorded in the Sermon on the Plain, which seems (as I said last Sunday) to have been a repetition of the substance, with certain variations as addressed to a somewhat different audience, of the Sermon on the Mount recorded by S. Matthew:

"Blessed be ye poor, for yours is the kingdom of God.

"Blessed are ye that hunger now, for ye shall be filled.

"Blessed are ye that weep now, for ye shall laugh.

"Blessed are ye when men shall hate you, and when they shall separate you from their company, and shall reproach you, and cast out your name as evil, for the Son of Man's sake. Rejoice ye in that day, and leap for joy: for behold your reward is great in Heaven: for in the like manner did their fathers unto the prophets."[1]

And then follows the contrast:

---

[1] S. Luke vi. 20–23.

But "Woe unto you when all men shall speak well of you; for in the same manner did their fathers unto the false prophets."

I. With reference to the Woe which we are to consider to-day, a comparison of the balancing and antithetical Blessing is specially important; for it at once shows that the Woe on Worldly Popularity is uttered in no misanthropic spirit of mere contempt for the opinion of others. The reproach, the evil-speaking, in which Christ bade His disciples rejoice, must arise for one cause only—"for righteousness sake," as S. Matthew gives the Beatitude, "for the Son of Man's sake," in S. Luke's version.

Note the exact expression. Our Lord does not simply say, "for My sake," in loyalty to Me as a personal Master. That would indeed have been sufficient. But He, as it were, explains and vindicates His claim to that loyalty, even in the face of persecution, by the title by which He describes Himself, "for the Son of Man's sake;" for the sake of the Ideal Man, in Whom righteousness is perfectly realized.

It is for loyalty to this pattern, for faithfulness to this revelation, and for that alone, that persecution or reproach is to be prized. There is no sort of encouragement given by our Lord's words to a wilful setting at nought of others' opinions, still less to a heedless incurring of odium, which may only be the token of pride and self-assertion at once intolerant and intolerable. Our Religion ought to recommend us to others, and we should recommend it. So in the face of heathen suspicion believers in Christ are warned by S. Peter, "Let none of you suffer as an evildoer, or as a busybody;"[1] they are bidden to have their behavior seemly among all, that with well-doing they might put to silence the ignorance of foolish and malicious men.[2] We are to take care that our good be not evil spoken of.[3] Christian slaves were expressly bidden to adorn the doctrine of God our Saviour in all things.[4] Christian women wedded to unbelieving husbands without the Word were to win their spouses to the faith of Christ by their own chaste and gentle conduct.[5] Christian clergy must have a good report of them that are without;[6] giving no offence in anything, but in all things approving themselves as the ministers of Christ.[7]

Of Jesus our Lord we are told that in His boyhood and youth He increased as in wisdom and stature so in favor both with God and

---

[1] 1 Pet. iv. 15.
[2] 1 Pet. ii. 12, 15.
[3] Rom. xiv. 16.
[4] Tit. ii. 10.
[5] 1 Pet. iii. 1.
[6] 1 Tim. iii. 7.
[7] 2 Cor. vi. 3, 4.

man.¹ When He entered on His ministry all wondered at His gracious words.² The people were drawn to Him, and on two occasions at least would have made Him their king had He been willing.³ They welcomed Him to Jerusalem at the last Passover with enthusiasm. It was His popularity which stirred the chief priests' envy and led them to plot His death.⁴

It is not then, mark you, absolutely, "Woe unto you when men speak well of you." There is a human favor which if we are not actually to seek it, we certainly must take care that we do nothing to forfeit. S. Paul made himself all things to all men that he might win some to Christ.⁵ Our Lord worked a miracle to provide the tribute money to avoid offending the Jews, who would not recognize or understand His claim to exemption from the tax.⁶ Of Daniel his enemies said, "We shall not find any occasion against this Daniel, except we find it against him concerning the law of his God."⁷ More than this we may be quite sure there is something wrong if *all* speak ill of us; if our religion does not make us lovable.

My brethren, is it so, we may well ask, with us, in our family and household circle, with our friends, with those with whom we have

---

¹ S. Luke ii. 52.   ² S. Luke iv. 22.
³ S. John vi. 15; xii. 13.   ⁴ S. Matt. xxvii. 18.
⁵ 1 Cor. ix. 22.   ⁶ S. Matt. xvii. 27.   ⁷ Dan. vi. 5.

business relations and contact? Are we free from blame save for our religion? And are we adorning that religion? The Christian believer surely should be one who can be relied on in all the relations of life for integrity and honor, for faithfulness and diligence, for courtesy and gentleness, for unselfishness and courage. Our religion must certainly be no sort of excuse for a disagreeable manner or disobliging temper, or for the neglect of ordinary duties. The reproach on which a blessing is promised is only that which comes "for the Son of Man's sake." Reproach deserved is not reproach "for righteousness sake." Persecution that we bring on ourselves is, one might say, no persecution. Persecution is that which comes on us because we are living true to God, without our having done anything to provoke it. Persecution and reproach must be neither sought nor provoked. As in the early days of the Church's conflict with the Roman Empire, when subject to open persecution, the faithful were forbidden to offer themselves for martyrdom or to court persecution, so must it always be. Persecution is to be allowed to come; and we are to be prepared for it. For it will surely come.

II. Hitherto I have been guarding against a misinterpretation of our Lord's words—not

I think without reason. But what do they mean? He does not say, "Woe unto you when men speak well of you." Human judgment we are not altogether to despise. The good are to approve. He does say, "Woe unto you when *all* men speak well of you." We are in the midst of a fallen world—a "naughty world," as our Prayer Book more than once happily phrases it—a world ruled by untrue principles, with false standards, dominated by a lying and deceiving spirit.[1] The majority of men, the mass of mankind, are not ruled by the Spirit of God. Their standards are different from those which Christ set up. Their Beatitudes differ from those which He pronounced. A pleasure-loving, selfish, proud, ambitious world cannot but dislike, fear, hate the really Christian character described in the Beatitudes of Jesus Christ, the temper of mind which thinks little of the world's greatest prizes, which longs for that which it contemns. Such a character and temper must expect the world's censure and scorn. The question is not, How shall we, if true to Christ, incur odium and reproach? But rather, How shall we not?

The Book of Wisdom describes the attitude

---

[1] S. John xiv. 30 ; 2 Cor. iv. 4 ; 1 S. John v. 19.

of the world toward the righteous man. When he is seen, the world will say of him:

"He is not for our turn, he is clean contrary to our doings. He was made to reprove our thoughts. He is grievous unto us even to behold: for his life is not like other men's, his ways are of another fashion."[1]

The world resents, quite naturally, that which by raising another and higher standard condemns its own practice. "Everyone that doeth evil hateth the light, neither cometh to the light, lest his deeds should be reproved."[2] Accordingly our Lord explained to His disciples the reason of the enmity which they were to be prepared to meet with from the world. "If ye were of the world, the world would love his own; but because ye are not of the world, but I have chosen you out of the world, therefore the world hateth you."[3] You know it, my brethren. The offence of the Cross has not ceased. All that will live godly in Christ Jesus, now as in the days of the Apostles, must be prepared to suffer persecution. The form of the conflict may be changed. Distinctive Christianity must be regarded by society people, by the club lounger, with dislike, with hatred. The Christian

---

[1] Wisd. ii. 12 sq.   [2] S. John iii. 20.
[3] S. John xv. 19, 20; cf. 1 S. John iv. 5, 6.

is called to live for nobler aims, by a stricter and more lofty standard, as well as with more inspiring motives than the world recognizes. He will be regarded as over-particular, straight-laced, narrow, and unpractical. The preaching of Christian doctrine, of the necessity of mortification, of the emptiness of worldly goods must ever be unpopular. In one sense a degenerate Christendom will resent the preaching of the truth more keenly than the Pagan world, for it will have an uneasy feeling that it has fallen from its true ideal.

III. We see then perhaps more clearly the force and application of our Lord's words. They teach us certainly this, to distrust the world's good opinion, to be suspicious of ourselves if there be not some element in us which provokes its resentment. General popularity was that which was given, our Lord says, to the False Prophets, to such as consented to prophesy not right things, but to speak smooth things, and prophesy deceits.[1] You will remember the story in the Book of Kings of Zedekiah the son of Chenaanah and the false prophets who encouraged Ahab to go up to Ramoth-gilead, and of Micaiah the son of Imlah, who was hated by King Ahab, because

---

[1] Isa. xxx. 10.

he did not prophesy good things concerning him.[1] The applause and favor of the world is always given to that which is on the side of the world. The false prophets were popular because they said what they were wanted to say. They gave a sort of religious sanction to the follies of the people, they made things easy. And then they passed away, leaving little mark behind them. They are contrasted with the true prophets, those who really spoke in the name of the Lord, who in their life were met with persecution, reproach, reviling. Such was Elijah.[2] Such were those commemorated in the list of Old Testament worthies in the Epistle to the Hebrews, "who had trials of cruel mockings and scourgings, of bonds and imprisonments; who were stoned, sawn asunder, tried, slain with the sword, of whom the world was not worthy."[3] Such has been the treatment of Prophets of God—forthtellers of His truth, proclaimers of His mind and will—in every age. They are, like scientific discoverers or great political reformers, before their time, above their fellows. And because they attack vested interests and vested prejudices they incur the odium of those who do not wish to be disturbed.

---

[1] 1 Kings xxii.   [2] 1 Kings xviii. 17, 18; xxi. 20.
[3] Heb. xi. 36–38.

The Prophets of God are persecuted during their earthly life. But their names live on in honor. After generations build their sepulchres.[1] We must learn to appeal from man's judgment, partial, imperfect, superficial, to God's Who tries the reins and the heart; and learn too to appeal from man's judgment now while so uninformed, to his judgment calm and impartial in history, or in the last great day. The world builds the sepulchres of the Prophets whom during their life it slighted; it raises memorials in their honor. You will gain respect by acting independently, by brave adherence to principle, as most certainly you will forfeit it by truckling to public opinion. What more fatal snare than Popularity-hunting for the writer, who writes down to the people; for the statesman, who dares not withstand the temporary current of opinion? The fate of such is a fulfilment in the lower sphere of our Lord's words, "Woe unto you when all men speak well of you, for so did their fathers unto the false prophets." It has been remarked[2] as a singular feature in the career of the lamented Dr. Lightfoot, the Bishop of Durham, that " he was one of the few

---

[1] S. Matt. xxiii. 29.
[2] By Archdeacon Farrar in a Memorial Notice of Bishop Lightfoot in the *Contemporary Review* for February, 1890.

who all his life long seems to have escaped from the stings of malice and detraction. Many public men of the present day, as in all ages, have lived for years amid incessant attacks of which they themselves are often unable to account for the bitterness. In not a few it happens, and has happened, to spend their lives in 'the oppression of a perpetual hissing.' Take the case of four of the most prominent divines of latter days, Dr. Pusey, Canon Kingsley, Professor Maurice, and Dean Stanley. Their personal experience would have led them to ratify the verdict of the Laureate,

> 'Each man walks with his head in a cloud of poisonous flies.'

During many years Dr. Pusey passed through hurricanes of abuse. Canon Kingsley, as he tells us in one of his letters, was at more than one period of his career 'cursed like a dog' in the public prints, and the chief religious newspaper of the day said of his strong and tender story 'Yeast,' that 'he taught immorality and insinuated Atheism.'" And, the writer goes on to say, in speaking of Bishop Lightfoot's singular felicity in escaping antagonism, "it is a blessed lot for those by whom it is won legitimately and without compromise. But if anyone be led to seek it by unhallowed means—by steering between the Scylla and Charybdis of Yes and No—or acquiring a reputation for safety and moderation by never stating a proposition without carefully protecting himself from seeming to exclude the contradictory—he is not following the great Bishop's example. Whatever be the rare exceptions, Christ's rule holds all but universally true, 'Woe unto you when all men shall speak well of you.' The rule is normal. Every now and then we seem to see exceptions."[1]

Let me give three practical rules by way of applying what has been said:

1. *Do not seek for popularity.* That is, never set this before you as an end. If all were right, if all had eyes to see and ears to hear, it ought

---

[1] I may be allowed to quote the following from an article on "The late Dean of S. Paul's," from the *Guardian* of December 17, 1890: "We are told to be on our guard when 'all men speak well of us;' and rightly; for no situation can be more morally perilous. Yet now and again we are allowed the privilege of seeing and loving characters who are so far removed from all taint of the perils of popularity that they can be safely permitted to receive the tribute of universal and unbroken praise, and to move, in flawless serenity, along a path which few could tread unharmed. It was so with Richard William Church. Not a breath of anger, not a word of blame, not a sound of wrangling criticism breaks the silence round his quiet grave in the green uplands of his Somersetshire village."

to follow, just as pleasure should follow the right exercise of any of our faculties, and in a perfectly healthy condition of body and mind will follow. Accept it, be grateful for it, if it comes. But never make it an end.

2. *Be always ready to sacrifice it.* That is, to use it. Continually we are tempted for fear of losing influence to shrink from using it. The words of Mordecai to Esther are always applicable: "Who knoweth whether thou didst not come to the kingdom for such a time as this?"[1] For what is influence or favor given if not to be used—and if necessary sacrificed. We must go forward like Esther. "If I perish, I perish."

3. *Distrust popularity.* It is not worth much. It is so vain and evanescent.

"Hosanna now, to-morrow Crucify
The changeful burden still of their rude, lawless cry."[2]

Jesus our Lord, Who knew what was in man would not commit Himself to men.[3]

Always and everywhere Public Opinion must needs contain certain, perhaps considerable, elements of truth. But we cannot surrender ourselves to it, defer to it absolutely.

---

[1] Esth. iv. 14.
[2] *Christian Year* for the First Sunday in Advent.
[3] S. John ii. 24, 25.

For consider how this Public Opinion is formed: it is practically the result of a general subscription; it is the workmanship of all the human beings who go to make up society or a section of society. The wise, the experienced, the conscientious, the disinterested, contribute toward it. But also the reckless, the unprincipled, the foolish, the selfish, have their share in producing it, a larger share, the world being what it is, than their nobler rivals.[1]

4. And one word for Lent. We are called to withdraw at this time from the distractions of society, to enter into our chamber and commune with our own heart and be still, to judge ourselves by the true standard. We will pray, "Try Thou me, O God, and seek Thou the ground of my heart."[2]

And lest we should incur this Woe pronounced by our Lord on Worldly Popularity,

> "Pray we our Lord, one pang to send
> Of deep, remorseful fear
> For every smile of partial friend.—
> Praise be our Penance here."[3]

---

[1] *Christ's Service and Public Opinion*, in Dr. Liddon's 2d Series of University Sermons, p. 160.

[2] Ps. cxxxix. 23.

[3] Mr. Keble's *Lyra Innocentium*, "Danger of Praise."

III.

THE WOE ON THE ABUSE OF RELIGIOUS PRIVILEGES.

"Then began he to upbraid the cities wherein most of his mighty works were done, because they repented not:

"Woe unto thee, Chorazin! woe unto thee, Bethsaida! for if the mighty works which were done in you had been done in Tyre and Sidon, they would have repented long ago in sackcloth and ashes.

"But I say unto you, It shall be more tolerable for Tyre and Sidon at the day of judgment, than for you.

"And thou, Capernaum, which art exalted unto heaven, shalt be brought down to hell: for if the mighty works, which have been done in thee, had been done in Sodom, it would have remained until this day. But I say unto you, It shall be more tolerable for the land of Sodom in the day of judgment, than for thee."—S. MATT. xi. 20–24.

CONCERNING this great rhythmic Woe, as it has been called, the Woe on the Abuse of Religious Privileges, there are two or three preliminary points that we shall do well to note before going on to consider the great moral law of God's dealings therein declared, and its application to ourselves.

1. The words are recorded both by S. Matthew and by S. Luke, but in a different connection. In S. Matthew they follow immediately on our Lord's upbraiding of the people for their rejection alike of John the Baptist and of Himself, although He and His precursor appealed to men's consciences by such very different methods. From John the ascetic prophet they turned away as from a gloomy demoniac — he was too severe — "he hath a devil." The Son of Man, Who entered into freer intercourse with the people, and sought to commend His words to their acceptance by His sweetness and affability, they accused of laxity. "Behold a gluttonous man and a winebibber, a friend of publicans and sinners." This incident would naturally recall to S. Matthew the other words in which our Lord "upbraided the cities where most of His mighty works were done, because they repented not."

But S. Luke directly connects the utterance of the Woe with the Mission of the Seventy Disciples whom our Lord, late in His ministry, shortly before His final approach to Jerusalem, sent before His face into every city and place whither He Himself was about to come.[1] And this would seem with little doubt to be the

---

[1] See S. Luke x. 1-20.

real historical setting of the utterance. The words have about them something of the nature of a Farewell, or at least of a final solemn warning, when our Lord's work in this part of the country was practically finished. "The harvest is past, the summer is ended, and ye are not saved."[1] "Woe unto thee, Chorazin! woe unto thee, Bethsaida! for if the mighty works had been done in Tyre and Sidon, which have been done in you, they had a great while ago repented, sitting in sackcloth and ashes."

2. It is remarkable that we have *no miracles recorded* in any of the Four Gospels as having been worked at either Chorazin or Bethsaida,[2] where Jesus says so many mighty works had been wrought. Now this is noticeable for two reasons:

a. It is a good illustration of the fragmentary character of the Gospel narratives. They do not profess, singly or together, to give a *whole* "Life of Christ." They are rather four "Memoirs." Sayings and doings of His are recorded such as had specially impressed themselves on the minds of His disciples; or such as each Evangelist selected from the mass

---

[1] Jer. viii. 20.

[2] The Bethsaida (Julias) of S. Mark vi. 45 was almost certainly a different place.

of material at his disposal as being particularly suitable for his special purpose. You will remember the concluding words of S. John's Gospel: "There are also many other things which Jesus did, the which if they should be written every one, I suppose that even the world itself could not contain the books that should be written:" a bold hyperbolical expression if taken literally, but answering to a deep truth, for a complete account of the perfect human life of the Lord would be practically infinite.[1]

b. Then, also, the absence from the narrative of the miracles referred to in this utterance of our Lord is a valuable though incidental witness, all the more valuable because incidental, to the genuineness of the Gospels. Had the story been legendary most assuredly it would not have been so artless. Jesus would not be represented as selecting the names of places which the writer had not connected with the legend.[2]

3. A third point of this kind I would call your attention to, the *literal fulfilment* of our Lord's denunciation. The very sites of Bethsaida and Chorazin cannot be fixed with cer-

---

[1] So Westcott on S. John xxi. 25.
[2] See Edersheim, *Life and Times of Jesus the Messiah*, Vol. II., p. 138.

tainty. Probably they were smaller cities, suburbs as we might say, one on each side, north and south, of Capernaum. Of Capernaum itself a writer says, " Standing on a vast field of ruin and upturned stones which marks the site of the modern *Tell Hum*, we feel that no description could be more pictorially true than that in which Christ prophetically likened the city in its downfall to the desolateness of death and Hades."[1]

This last observation leads to the remark that our Lord's words are apparently to be understood as having reference, primarily at any rate, to the *temporal* punishment and destruction that would come upon these *cities* in *their* day of judgment and visitation, as upon Sodom and Gomorrah, upon Tyre and Sidon, in earlier ages, rather than to the *eternal* destruction of the *souls* of their inhabitants. "There is, it is important to remember, a visitation of vengeance or the contrary, on nations, cities, tribes, even families in *this* life, which is quite irrespective of the *eternal* award on individual souls."[2] We are by no means bound to suppose that all who perished in the Flood, or in the overthrow of the Cities of the Plain, or in later judicial catastrophes,

---

[1] Edersheim, II., 139.
[2] Rev. M. F. Sadler, *Commentary on S. Matthew, in loc.*

were eternally lost. Rather we may hope that in many cases the destruction of the flesh was for the saving of the spirit in the day of the Lord Jesus.[1]

At the same time, of course, this temporal punishment and ruin was a type and foreshadowing of the last great Day of Judgment when all accounts shall be settled, "the day of wrath and revelation of the righteous judgment of God, who will render to every man according to his deeds."[2] It was such a type because it was an illustration of a general law of God's dealing, of the absolute justice of God's dealings with all. That Justice contains within itself the element of Mercy; for it takes all circumstances into account. Think of it.

"Tyre and Sidon had their full share of the degradations which in all ages have been the curse of seaport towns, and their religion, instead of doing anything to raise them, was of a character still further to degrade and brutalize them. The Phœnician worship of Nature in the form which it took in these ancient cities was little better than a prolonged, though disguised, appeal to the worst appetites of cruelty and lust. And yet, as our Lord surveyed the towns on or near the brink

---

[1] See 1 Cor. v. 5.   [2] Rom. ii. 5, 6.

of the Sea of Galilee—Chorazin and Bethsaida—and considered how in them, as the ruins of the synagogue of the neighboring Capernaum attest at this hour, the worship of the true God was splendidly provided for, and how again and again each of them had listened to His teaching and had witnessed His miracles, He uttered one of the most startling judgments of the Gospel. If the degraded pagans of the Phœnician seaboard had only had the advantages of the favored Galilean towns, they would long ago have turned with deep, heart-searching penitence to God."[1]

Here you see is the great moral law declared, that *Judgment is according to Opportunities.* This is to be laid to heart both for consolation and for warning.

I. The Judge of all the earth will most assuredly, we know, do right.[2] We are troubled and perplexed sometimes when we think of the multitudes of the heathen to whom the knowledge of God in Jesus Christ has not been vouchsafed, of the number of people round about us who are strangers to the Catholic Faith. Am I to regard all such as inevitably lost because they believe not? Most certainly not. Judgment is according to op-

---

[1] From a Sermon of Dr. Liddon's at S. Paul's Cathedral.
[2] Gen. xviii. 25.

portunity. There are the many stripes for those who knew and did not their Lord's will, the few stripes for those who did it not because they knew it not.[1] "He that believeth and is baptized shall be saved: but he that *disbelieveth* shall be condemned."[2] Erase, I pray you, the erroneous translation of the Authorized Version, "he that believeth not." There is a wide difference between a position of negative unbelief and that of positive disbelief. The original implies active, not merely negative unbelief. It is he who *rejecteth* the Gospel when it is fairly brought before him, refusing belief and obedience, who is condemned. And this, remember, involves a good deal more than mere local contiguity. There may be inherited prejudices, a practical want of opportunity, the absence of a fair presentation, which in God's judgment excuse many whom we might be tempted to condemn as unbelievers. To speak thus is not, I would beg you to note, to say that one religion is as good as another, or, in the language of one of our Articles of Religion,[3] that every man shall be saved by the Law or Sect which he professeth, so that he be diligent to frame his life according to that Law and the light of Nature.

---

[1] S. Luke xii. 47, 48.   [2] S. Mark xvi. 16.
[3] Art. XVIII.

"Holy Scripture doth set out unto us only the Name of Jesus Christ, whereby men must be saved." But the question is, How and when men may be brought into saving union with Christ? The Sacraments of the Church are the ordinary and appointed channels of grace. But because we are tied to their use God is not tied to use no other means. His grace can overflow its accustomed banks. And we may well hope with regard to those who have been true, amid whatever imperfections, to the light which the Word, who is the light of every man that cometh into the world,[1] hath given, that He has means in another world of communicating to them the fulness of Christian grace and truth, the light of the Incarnate Word which here they had not known.

God, we are sure, will reject none who do not reject Him. He will lose none whom He can save.

II. Along with the consolation and encouragement suggested by the knowledge that judgment is and will be according to opportunity, there is for warning a corresponding axiom: From them to whom much is given shall much be required.[2] God does not expect to reap where He has not sown, or to gather

---

[1] S. John i. 9.   [2] S. Luke xii. 48.

where He has not strawed. But He does look to reap where and as He has sown.¹ The more opportunity, the greater the responsibility. The greater the privileges, the more abundant should be the fruit. We are so apt to rest in privileges. The Jewish boast, "We be Abraham's seed," ² is continually repeated by Christian believers. The question for us is, What is our faith doing for us? What is it enabling us to do and bear? Do we live by faith? Are we building up ourselves, our moral and spiritual life, on the foundation of our most holy faith? As members of the Christian Church are we, in correspondence with the twofold meaning and derivation of the word,³ seen to be separated from the world, living by a higher standard, with higher aims, by a higher power, because we are united with the Lord, living members of His mystical Body, animated and quickened by His Spirit? As claiming fellowship through an unbroken line of ministry with the Apostles do we manifest a moral kinship with those whom we claim as spiritual ancestors? Do we show in our lives the transforming power of Sacraments as real means of grace—not charms? Many, we are warned,

---

¹ S. Matt. xxv. 24.   ² S. John viii. 33.
³ Ἐκκλησία, called out of the World ; κυριακή, dedicated to the Lord.

will say, "Lord, Lord, we have eaten and drunk in Thy presence, Thou hast taught in our streets, we have even done many wonderful works in Thy name," to whom the Lord will reply, "Depart from me, I never knew you, ye workers of iniquity."[1]

Are we to be indifferent, then, for ourselves or for others to the privileges which are offered? God forbid. We must use them to the uttermost. We cannot, if we would, make ourselves as the heathen.[2] "The Word that I have spoken, it shall judge you at the last day."[3] Nor dare we in a cowardly and ungenerous fashion hold back from seeking to win others to what we prize for ourselves. Not with scorn or disdain but with love and pity will we regard those who are without. They lose so much. Their life is so much poorer. They are deprived of what would give strength in temptation, consolation in trouble, a brighter hope for the future.

Two thoughts, one doctrinal and one personal, let me suggest in conclusion.

(1) In this comparison between Chorazin and Bethsaida on the one side, and Tyre and Sidon on the other, mark the claim of Jesus

---

[1] S. Matt. vii. 21-23.   [2] Ezek. xx. 32.
[3] S. John xii. 48.

Christ to the possession of absolute and perfect knowledge, in a word, to Divine Omniscience. We instinctively appeal from man's fallible, superficial, partial opinion to the unerring, penetrating judgment of Almighty God. It is right that we should do so. We considered this last Sunday. But Jesus Christ claims not only to award the due recompense, the final doom for weal or woe to all; He claims, moreover, to know how they would have acted, what each would have been, in other circumstances than those with which God actually surrounded them. Is such language, we can but ask, consistent with intellectual modesty, with real moral goodness in any merely created being? Do not the words furnish an evidence of His Divine Nature and Person? This thought I have often developed; I need not now expand it; but I would ask you seriously to consider it.

(2) Jesus Christ knows what we could not know, whether you or I would do better or worse than we do, if we were placed by Him in other than our present circumstances. He knows this, because He knows our inmost dispositions and sees us as we are. We are often tempted to think that if only our lot had been cast in some other age or amid different surroundings, the battle would have been so much easier. It is an idle thought. We shall

be—we are—judged by Him according to our works, and according to our opportunities, in our actual circumstances, all of which He perfectly understands. "I know thy works," He says, "and where thou dwellest."[1] May He then give us grace to use the grace, to correspond with the opportunities that He affords.

---

[1] Rev. ii. 13.

IV.

THE WOE ON OFFENCES.

"Woe unto the world because of offences! for it must needs be that offences come; but woe to that man by whom the offence cometh!"—S. MATTHEW xviii. 7.

IN treating this Woe (recorded, it is worth while to remember, in each of the three earlier Gospels[1]) it can hardly be necessary to explain that "offence," the noun, and "offend," the verb, in New Testament language refer not to *a wrong done to us,* in the ordinary sense, but to something *by which we are led to do wrong,* though this is indeed the greatest wrong that can be done to us. An offence is a stumbling-block; to offend is to put a stumbling-block in another's path. So the verse that I read is better translated, for modern ears at any rate, in the Revised Version:

"Woe unto the world because of occasions of stumbling! for it must needs be that the occasions come; but woe to that man through whom the occasion cometh!"

---

[1] With the text compare S. Mark ix. 42; S. Luke xvii. 1.

I. With this understanding of the words who will wonder at the utterance of this Woe by our Lord—both as a lamentation and as a denunciation, in sorrow and in judgment? Why, that which He laments and denounces is the very hindrance and obstacle to the work He came to do. He came as a Moral Reformer; to raise the fallen, to cheer the sorrowful, to heal the wounded, to abolish sin, to give or restore health, moral and spiritual well-being. That we "might have life, and have it more abundantly,"[1] for this He gave His life, in toil, in poverty, in witness, in wrestling with evil. He is the Saviour, from sin, mind you, from moral evil, which is the real and fundamental cause of sorrow and misery in the world; He is the Restorer of true health.[2] And over against Him is one whose name is "the Destroyer," the angel of the abyss, a murderer from the beginning, the prince of this world.[3]

"Alas! alas!" the Saviour cries, "for the World under the rule, so cruel and so crafty, of its wily Prince, who murders through his lies, casting a glamour over his victims, covering so skilfully his stumbling-blocks, baiting so attractively his snares. In the World, so fallen, so ruled, causes of stumbling, occa-

---

[1] S. John x. 10.   [2] S. Matt. i. 21.
[3] Rev. ix. 11.; S. John viii. 44; xiv. 30.

sions of sin, must needs be! but Woe," He adds, and here surely He speaks not in sympathy but in judgment, "Woe to that man through whom the occasion cometh!"

Such an one, whether consciously or unconsciously, is doing the Devil's work. He is used by Satan as a tool and agent in his work of destruction. Think of it, my brethren; whenever you or I have tempted another to do wrong, in whatever way, put a stumbling-block, of whatever kind, in another's path, we were doing the Devil's work; we were doing our part to frustrate the work of Jesus Christ, Who "was manifested to destroy the works of the Devil." [1]

The Church as the Body, the Spouse, of Christ is to further His interests, to carry on His healing, saving work. The World, as the Harlot, the slave of the Evil One is used by him as his tool in his work of moral destruction. [2]

No wonder then, I say, that the Saviour pronounced this Woe; that He declared in words that immediately precede the text, "Whoso shall cause to stumble one of these little ones—children in years or innocence, or weak believers—it were better for him that a great millstone—not the ordinary light stone

---

[1] 1 S. John iii. 8.
[2] See the contrast in Rev. xvii. and xix.

used by women in grinding, but a larger stone drawn by an ass—should be hanged about his neck, and that he should be sunk in the depths of the sea."

Such a death was not a recognized punishment according to the Jewish Law; but it was in occasional use, for great criminals, among both Greeks and Romans. It is said that the Romans had inflicted the punishment, not long before, on some in Galilee, perhaps on some of the ringleaders of the insurrection under Judas of Galilee. Our Lord's words would then have come home with a special vividness to the minds of His hearers. The infamy He would mean of causing to stumble morally, of leading into sin, a single "little one" belonging to Him was as great as that of those whose crimes brought on them this exceptional punishment. It would be better rather than incur this guilt to be plunged into the depths of the sea. The peculiar horror of the punishment, both for Jews and heathen, consisted in this, that the body thus weighted, when plunged into deep water, could not possibly be rescued for burial, and the absence of burial rites was supposed to affect the condition of the soul.

II. Now before we consider some of the different ways in which we may incur this Woe, I would ask you to notice a point of contact, and to a certain extent of collision, with some modern ideas presented by these words of our Lord. He shows Himself, if I may so speak, abreast of modern thought so far as *facts* are concerned; while His words reprove a certain *inference* which men are sometimes tempted to draw from those facts.

"The two clauses 'It must needs be that occasions of stumbling come,' 'but woe unto that man through whom the occasion cometh,' unite (it has been well said[1]) in strange contrast the two truths which all the history of human guilt brings before us. Crimes seem to run with something like the inevitable regularity of a law, and yet in each single instance the will of the offender has been free to choose, and he is therefore rightly held responsible both by Divine and human laws."

Some modern philosophers point us to the existence of sin in the mass; they claim to be able to estimate the average amount of crime, and of different crimes, by statistics: then they would infer from this that there is in reality no such thing as Freedom of Will, that what we call "sins" are merely the natural results of circumstances—of heredity and environment

---

[1] Dean Plumptre, in Ellicott's *N. T. Commentary for English Readers*, on the text. See also Dean Mansel in *The Speaker's Commentary*. Compare Luthardt, *Saving Truths of Christianity*, Lect. II., p. 71.

and so forth ; they deny any responsibility for our actions.

Against such a theory, of course, any healthy conscience rebels, whether or no we be able to answer the intellectual problem. We *know* that our actions have been our own, that we did them, that we consented to the suggestion, whether of good or evil, made it our own, executed it. We hold ourselves responsible, unless we have played tricks on our moral instincts. But it is well to see the intellectual fallacy of the argument.

Now the kind of law, if it may be so called, which is established by such statistical calculations is of a totally different kind from those natural laws which indicate an unvarying sequence of cause and effect. These are based on induction. The law is inferred from a generalization, from its observance being noticed in all known individual cases. But the other kind of law, the law of criminal statistics, is altogether different. Here all that we have are statements of general uniformity observed in masses only, and not in individuals. The individual variations are lost sight of owing to the large scale on which the calculation is made. But it is in the individual that the operation of the will is found to be influenced by grace, refined by a nobler, better motive, that it rises from a lower to a higher level, or sinks from a truer to a poorer standard of life.

Woe, then, to the world because of offences! "Through man's abuse of his free will such offences have ever been, ever will be, in this world of trial. But they are a heavy woe to the world, on whom they come; they are a heavier woe to the man, through whom they come."[1]

III. To pass on. There are three chief ways, it seems to me, in which a person may cause others to stumble, and so incur this Woe, *three groups*, so to speak, *of stumbling-blocks*, or causes of offence.

1. Worst of all are those cases in which a person deliberately sets himself to trip another, to lead him into sin ; or at least wantonly takes the risk of doing so. This may be in various ways, with various motives.

An accomplice may be necessary—for different kinds of wrong-doing ; or it may be hoped by another's aid more easily to escape detection ; or the very sense of being unlike to others may lead to the desire to make them like one's self ; or with more or less heartlessness persons may repudiate any responsibility for the possible effect of their example or

---

[1] Dr. Pusey, in a sermon on "Murder of Souls" in his *University and Cathedral Sermons*, p. 364.

conduct on others. "If others choose to take offence, or to be influenced by me, that is their concern, not mine; am I my brother's keeper?"

In London there is a famous exhibition—dear to children, visited probably by some of you—Madame Tussaud's Waxworks, where life-size and life-like representations are found of all the celebrities of the world—royal personages, statesmen, generals, and such like—and criminals. For there is a separate room called "The Chamber of Horrors," where figures are preserved of notorious murderers (the heads taken, I believe, from casts made after execution), whose crimes and trials have excited widespread interest. Here, for instance, is the cold-blooded murderer who allured his victim to some lonely spot, and then fell on him and slaughtered him, for plunder and rapine. There is a calculating poisoner, with perhaps a whole group of victims. My brethren, may we not recognize with a shudder the counterpart of such criminals in soul-murderers? Does conscience whisper to any, "Thou mightest have a place, in the sight of Heaven, in such a spiritual Chamber of Horrors?"

Look. Here is a seducer who has set himself to work the ruin of the innocent object of his passion. He plots, he bribes, he hides his hand, and at last he accomplishes his purpose. A soul is killed; a character is lost; physical consequences are perhaps involved. And then—is he responsible for anything that may follow?

But the gratification of passion is not the only incentive to such blood-guiltiness. For the gratification of vanity, or for filthy lucre's sake, men and women will write that which will bring them money or fame, with little regard to the effect on the faith or life of their readers. Here is a vain person with a certain power of thought and of expression. He will write something startling—original perhaps he would call it. It is sometimes a cheap way of earning a reputation for smartness to pour ridicule on the belief of others, to denounce all that has been acknowledged, and deny what has been generally affirmed. It will cause distress, of course, to many earnest souls, and rob of their comfort and stay some who have a hard fight; there will be a risk of shipwrecks of faith among persons of little stability, the "little ones" of whom Christ speaks; but what does that matter, or what concern is that for the writer? Only this, "Woe unto him through whom the cause of stumbling cometh!"

Let me give another illustration. There is a young girl who means no manner of evil.

Certainly not. But she "must have a little fun," she cannot refrain from a harmless flirtation; and if men are so evil that their passions are kindled, that they, when led on, get beyond their own control, is that her fault? Or if the extravagant following of a fashion in dress, which certainly cannot be said to be in exact agreement with the dictates of Christian modesty, should suggest evil to others—why, how—it is asked—can I be blamed?

Amid such self-justifying reasoning I hear the solemn tones of the Saviour's voice—Who is also the Judge of men—"Woe to that man, that woman, through whom the occasion of stumbling cometh."

2. Besides what may be called *Murder*, in the first or second degree, we sometimes have a verdict returned, not so often perhaps as should be the case, of *Culpable Negligence*, that amounts to Manslaughter, as the cause of some railroad disaster, or of some great conflagration, or of the collapse of a building through faulty construction. Is there not a corresponding sinful thoughtlessness and inconsiderateness with regard to others' moral and spiritual well-being?

We are continually challenged in these days to bring our religion to bear on matters of daily life, not to keep it as something for the

Church, but to let it enter into social and civil life. We, my brethren, who believe in the Incarnation can have no hesitation in accepting the challenge. For is it not the very law of the Incarnation, to bring to bear the highest motives and powers on the most ordinary commonplace matters? "The Word was made flesh, and dwelt among us."[1] I shall not then hesitate to apply our subject to questions of Trade and Business. Whatever may be our opinion or judgment upon certain theories and plans, we shall all recognize that there is a legitimate Christian Socialism, which is nothing but Christianity applied to the social order, and which is opposed alike to unchristian socialism and to unsocial Christians.

Well, then, you draw dividends, the highest you can get, from some railroad or other stocks. You are a sleeping partner (deeply slumbering perhaps) in some large business concern. Do you ever think it necessary to question how the company is able to pay these large dividends; whether the money is fair and legitimate profit; or whether it is wrung out through the payment of starvation wages, or by exacting hours of toil that practically give no opportunity for moral and spiritual improvement to the workers, who are regarded

---

[1] S. John i. 14.

simply as "hands" and nothing more? In your shopping do you persist in buying at the lowest possible, or impossible prices, and in patronizing stores where you know, or ought to know, that wages are given which are in no sense a fair recompense for the service rendered, nor a fair day's wage for a fair day's work? Are you not then in some degree responsible, with your theory of unrestricted competition, for the dishonorable ways of supplementing an income, of earning support for others beside herself perhaps, to which the poor girl is almost forced?

"Competition," said the late Frederick Denison Maurice in one of his prophet-like utterances, "is put forth as the law of the universe. That is a lie. The time is come for us to declare that it is a lie by word and deed."[1]

Or as an owner of property are you doing what you can to provide such proper house-room as may be a safeguard for morality and decency, or are you regardless of arrangements which are a direct temptation to vice? In these and such like matters are there not occasions of stumbling put in the way of those whom Christ calls His little ones, to which His words refer? All, through thoughtlessness. Yes, but we are taught in the

---

[1] *Life*, vol. ii., p. 32.

Litany to pray to our Lord—the Saviour and the Judge of men—for forgiveness of our sins, negligences, and ignorances—thoughtless sins, culpable negligences, inexcusable ignorance; and to pray, moreover, that by the aid of His Holy Spirit—of love and truth and wisdom—we may be enabled to amend our lives according to His Holy Word and standard. And what is that, but that we should think of, care for others as we would that others should take thought and care for us and for those who are dear to us?

3. One other kind of stumbling-block I must not pass by, although there can be no need to dwell on it at length, the sin is so common and so generally recognized—the stumbling-block of *Inconsistency*. The inconsistency of those "who profess and call themselves Christians," but whose lives give the lie to their profession, and whom others refuse to recognize as Christians, if the designation means disciples and followers of Jesus the Christ. How often we fail, my brethren, at any rate "to adorn the doctrine of God our Saviour in all things," to recommend it to others by our example![1] Alas, we not only fail to attract; we even repel. We ourselves *are* a stumbling-block in the way of others.

---

[1] Tit. ii. 10.

Continually does a clergyman, when pressing the claims of Christ upon someone's allegiance, or urging the importance and value of the Sacraments and the ordinances of religion, have this thrown in his face: "Church members are no better than other people; So and So has been confirmed, receives the Sacrament; but little good it does." Alas, alas! Woe to him through whom the occasion of stumbling cometh.

Not to speak of serious scandals, by our loss of temper, by a peevish, complaining spirit under trouble, by ill-concealed ambition, by our miserable rivalry, Christian believers, Church-people, clergymen, show how largely our affections are fixed on things temporal, often on things miserably petty, while we profess to be living in the light of a higher world.

The excuse is, I know, often exaggerated, always in a way unreasonable. Such inconsistencies, sad and distressing as they are, afford no real excuse to another for holding back. The abuse of religious privileges does not prove that there is no value in them. Rather a person's own sense of the inconsistency shows that he recognizes the true ideal; the abuse is a caution to him to be downright, thorough, and whole-hearted in his faith and obedience.

"The Scribes and the Pharisees," said our Lord to the people, "sit in Moses' seat; all things therefore whatsoever they bid you, these do and observe; but do not ye after their works, for they say, and do not." [1]

The consideration of such ways of causing others to stumble should surely, my brethren, be a call to self-examination, to humiliation, to earnest prayer. "Let not my brother, for whom Christ died, be destroyed through my sin." [2] "Have mercy, Lord, on all with whom I have at any time, in any way, shared in sin, whether by counsel or provocation, by example or co-operation. Grant that having sinned together we may together repent, and together find mercy with Thee, both now and at the last." [3]

It is not inappropriate to our subject that your offerings should be asked this morning toward the support of the Sisters of S. Margaret's Home.

Over against this Woe pronounced by our Lord on him who causes another to stumble, there is a Blessing written at the end of the Epistle of S. James. "My brethren," he says, "if any among you do err from the truth, and

---

[1] S. Matt. xxiii. 2, 3. [2] Rom. xiv. 15.
[3] See *Manual of Intercessory Prayer*, Collect 82; and Bp. Andrewes' *Devotions*, for the Second Day.

one convert him; let him know that he which converteth a sinner from the error of his way shall save a soul from death, and shall cover a multitude of sins."

The words are an encouragement and incentive to us all in any endeavor we may make —by prayers, by alms, by labor, by example, by the exertion of influence, by expostulation —for others' moral and spiritual well-being. The Church as a collective society is to carry on our Lord's saving work. The words may have a special application to those specially dedicated to God's service, whether in the Sacred Ministry or in what is called the Religious Life, giving themselves to works of mercy, both corporal and spiritual. Let me mention the chief works of this kind undertaken by the Sisters of S. Margaret's. In Boston, besides their Infirmaries and Embroidery Rooms, by which, while ministering to others' needs and working for the Sanctuary, they endeavor to support themselves, the Children's Hospital has been for eighteen years under their care, and they have the charge, and to a large extent the pecuniary responsibility for S. Monica's Home, a small hospital for colored people, for whom in regard of certain cases no provision is made in our larger hospitals. They have a large share in the work of S. Augustine's Mission, and give valued help in our Guilds and Sunday-School at St. John's. Outside of Boston they are established in five other large cities—in Washington, Philadelphia, Newark, Jersey City, and Montreal. In four of these places the Sisters do parish and mission work under the local clergy.[1] They have charge of two large Hospitals;[2] of two Penitentiary institutions;[3] and of two Homes for Sick or Aged People.[4]

In each place they form a centre for Christian work, of Christian influence and devotion. None of these different institutions is able to do more than provide for the support of the Sisters actually engaged in it; the expenses of the Mother House, where Sisters are trained, and where various incidental works of charity are carried on, have to be met by the Sisters themselves, with the aid of friends and of the faithful generally.

None I hope will be more conscious than those who wear a special uniform marking them out as dedicated to our Lord of the dan-

---

[1] At S. James's, Washington; S. Mark's, Philadelphia; the House of Prayer, Newark; S. John the Evangelist's, Montreal.

[2] S. Barnabas', Newark, and Christ Hospital, Jersey City.

[3] S. Katharine's Home, Jersey City, and S. Margaret's Nursery, Montreal.

[4] S. Mark's Home, Philadelphia, and S. Margaret's, Montreal.

ger of inconsistency and scandal. But amid whatever imperfections the Sisters' desire and intention is to devote themselves, after their Lord's example and for His sake, to carry on His work of mercy—helping, healing, restoring, saving.

I ask for them your liberal help. Some may be glad to make an offering as a loving act of reparation for occasions of stumbling that are remembered with sorrow in the past; some in gratitude for having themselves been preserved or rescued from falling. We all would show ourselves on the side not of the Destroyer but of the Saviour of mankind.

V.

THE WOE ON HYPOCRISY.

"Woe unto you, Scribes and Pharisees, hypocrites! for ye pay tithe of mint and anise and cummin, and have omitted the weightier matters of the law, judgment, mercy, and faith: these ought ye to have done, and not to leave the other undone.

"Ye blind guides, which strain at a gnat and swallow a camel!

"Woe unto you, Scribes and Pharisees, hypocrites! for ye make clean the outside of the cup and of the platter, but within they are full of extortion and excess.

"Thou blind Pharisee, cleanse first that which is within the cup and platter, that the outside of them may be clean also.

"Woe unto you, Scribes and Pharisees, hypocrites! for ye are like unto whited sepulchres, which indeed appear beautiful outward, but are within full of dead men's bones, and of all uncleanness.

"Even so ye also outwardly appear righteous unto men, but within ye are full of hypocrisy and iniquity."—S. MATTHEW xxiii. 23–28.

THE great series of seven or eight Woes on Hypocrisy set down in the twenty-third chapter of S. Matthew was uttered by our Lord on one of the earlier days in the Holy Week, apparently on the Tuesday before He suffered. At the end of the discourse He bade the Temple and its courts a solemn and sad farewell:

"O Jerusalem, Jerusalem, thou that killest the prophets, and stonest them which are sent unto thee, how often would I have gathered thy children together, even as a hen gathereth her chickens under her wings, and ye would not! Behold, your house is left unto you desolate. For I say unto you, Ye shall not see me henceforth, till ye shall say, Blessed is he that cometh in the name of the Lord;"[1] till, that is, they or their children should acknowledge Him as the Messiah, and welcome Him with a Hosanna more true and real than the empty cry of a day or two before.

The discourse then, with its context, falls in well with thoughts of Passion-tide. The occasion of its delivery is parallel to that other withdrawal from the Temple of which we hear in to-day's Gospel, when—a few months earlier—the Jews took up stones—the great stones that were lying about in the courts for the building of the Temple, which was still going on—to cast at our Lord for His claim to Divine Sonship and Pre-existence. "Jesus hid Himself and went out of the Temple," retiring before their fury.[2] It was when these

---

[1] Vv. 37-39. [2] S. John viii. 59.

words were read in the Gospel for this Sunday that of old the veil was drawn over the Cross above the Altar in penitent acknowledgment of the sins which drove away the Saviour, rejecting Him, and at the last killing Him.

The remembrance of the context and of the sorrowful lamentation over the Temple and the city tend, I think, to show that these Woes, like the others which we have considered, are not to be understood as simply denunciatory. Along with the judicial sentence on the sin there is mingled also a yearning compassion for those who are its victims—something of the passionate complaint that broke forth on another occasion, "Ye will not come to Me that ye might have life."[1] It has been suggested that "Woe *for* you" might be a better rendering of the words. "Woe unto you" seems to exclude too entirely the element of sorrow, as well as of indignation, of which the Greek interjection is at least capable.

These Woes are all called forth by and directed against the Hypocrisy of the Scribes and Pharisees—the ruling class, that is, of the Jewish Church. The Scribes, as learned in the Scriptures, claimed to interpret their mean-

---

[1] S. John v. 40.

ing. The Pharisees, by reason of their strict observance of the Law, were regarded as patterns for the people. Each clause begins with the words, "Woe unto you," or "Woe for you, Scribes and Pharisees, hypocrites!" with one variation, "Woe, ye blind guides!"

Woe for the Scribes and Pharisees, hypocrites—

(1) Woe on the abuse of the key of knowledge, by which instead of leading men to the truth they shut them out therefrom :

(2) Woe on the greedy cant, which under pretence of religion sponged on the simple folk :

(3) Woe on the proselytizing fanaticism, which aimed only at an outward conversion and not a change of heart :

(4) Woe on the blind guides, with their false, perverted casuistry :

(5) Woe on the sham scrupulosity which, with a total want of sense of proportion, was punctilious as to the infinitely little, to the disregard of the infinitely great :

(6) Woe on the hideous contrast between external spotlessness and inner corruption :

(7) Woe on the mock repentance which condemned their fathers for the murder of the prophets while they themselves reflected the murderous spirit of their fathers, and were about to condemn and crucify the Lord of the prophets.

Now, my brethren, it is an easy matter for us to condemn and ridicule the Pharisees and *their* hypocrisy. Very easy, I say, but not very profitable. In doing this we may be playing their very part, condemning those of a former age or of other circumstances while we are really guilty of the self-same sin, though with us and in our circumstances it may take a different shape. If we are to learn *our* lesson from these words of our Lord, from this Gospel Woe, we must look a little more closely into the nature of Hypocrisy.

"The Greek word translated 'Hypocrite' literally means an 'Actor,' one who plays a part or assumes a character. There are of course two classes of actors:

"First, those who act legitimately, who for the sake of affording amusement or instruction play a part upon the stage;

"Secondly, those who with the intent to deceive their neighbors play a part in actual life.

"In modern English the word 'Actor' is restricted to the first class, and the word 'Hypocrite' to the second; and a Hypocrite is used only in a bad sense, its original signification of playing a part or assuming a character has been forgotten."[1]

---

[1] Professor Momerie's Sermons on Cant, in his volume *Preaching and Hearing*, p. 207.

But this is the essence of Hypocrisy, in all its different forms, ancient and modern.

Now Hypocrites—those who profess what they do not feel, who assume a character outwardly to which there is nothing in the heart which corresponds—may be reckoned as belonging to two classes. Rather, for, knowing the deceitfulness of our own hearts, we will not speak in the third person, as if the matter did not concern ourselves, let us say, Hypocrisy is of two chief kinds, takes two leading forms:

I. There is *the acting a part before others*, deceiving the world;

II. There is *the acting a part before ourselves*, self-deceit.

Some would add a third form of Hypocrisy, *the acting a part before God;* but this, since it can hardly be conceived of as conscious and deliberate, we can better, perhaps, include under the head of Self-deceit. We are thinking throughout, you will understand, of Hypocrisy that is connected with Religion.

I. First, then, there is the acting a part before others. Of this kind of Hypocrisy there are many subdivisions. I can point to but a few.

1. There is the Mercenary Hypocrite who hopes by his profession of piety to enrich

himself. There were Pharisees who for a pretence made long prayers, and as soon as the prayers were over proceeded to devour widows' houses. Such have their counterpart in modern life. Downright rascality of this sort is not unknown. And in less glaring ways such hypocrisy is familiar among us.

2. But a more common form of Hypocrisy is that which seeks not Gain but Esteem and the good opinion of others. Such hypocrites know that genuine religion is admired, and they fancy that by merely appearing religious they may secure the admiration they desire. They want a reputation for piety. They hunger and thirst for esteem. They live on appreciation. And so "All their works they do to be seen of men." Now it is against anything of this sort that our Lord warns us repeatedly in the Sermon on the Mount. When we pray, fast, give alms, He bids us, "Be not as the actors," calling attention to our good deeds, our pious practices. They fast, they pray, they give alms, that they may be seen, appreciated, applauded of men. "Verily I say unto you, They have their reward." But thou, He says, when thou prayest, enter into thy chamber for thy spiritual exercises; call not attention to thy self-denial; with regard to alms and works of charity let not thy left hand know what thy right hand

doeth. Keep all such things as far as may be secret with God, for Whom they are intended. And thy Father, which seeth in secret, shall reward thee openly.[1]

We not only lose any true reward by such conduct as our Lord condemns; we suffer an interior loss and hurt. The effect of allowing such secondary motives to sway our conduct is to blind the heart and conscience. The pure in heart, with a single eye, alone can see God and the things of God. "How can ye believe which receive honor one from another, and seek not the honor which cometh from the only God?"[2] Accordingly, our Lord reproaches the hypocritical Scribes and Pharisees as "fools and blind." Their own moral perception is perverted.

II. And so we naturally come to the consideration of the second great variety of Hypocrisy—acting a part before ourselves—Self-deceit. This follows on the deceit of others.

The hypocrite constantly endeavors to appear that which he is not. At last he may even deceive himself. He may come to believe that he actually is what he has always been trying to appear to be.

"It is said that if actors were to play con-

---

[1] S. Matt. vi. 1-18.   [2] S. John v. 44.

tinually the same part night after night for many years, their minds might possibly become affected, so that at last they would get confused about their own identity, and scarcely be able to tell whether they were themselves or the characters they represented. Since the hypocrite acts not only in the evening, but all day long as well, there would seem to be even more likelihood of his being overtaken by a similar catastrophe."[1]

Here you see is a deeper danger, a dreadful Woe, to think ourselves religious when we have only the form of godliness, and are denying its restraining and transforming power. This is what our Lord points to in the case of the Pharisees, in various ways.

1. They had formulated a shrewd casuistry, by which it was proposed to keep the law in the letter and break it in the spirit. A good many instances of a similar false casuistry by which people seek to drug their consciences will suggest themselves to a thoughtful mind. Let me mention one, not so common perhaps to-day as a few years ago. There are people who would think it very wicked to open a newspaper on Sunday, who do not hesitate to spend a considerable time on the Lord's day in talking about the subjects of which they

---

[1] Momerie, p. 182.

would read in the paper, and perhaps about a good deal of personal gossip also.

2. Then there is the allied snare of being scrupulous and exact about petty details, while neglectful of weightier matters of the law. Tithing potherbs—mint, anise, cummin—and disregarding great ethical obligations—judgment, mercy, faith. A most glaring illustration we have of this in the history of the Passion. The chief priests and rulers of the people led our Lord on Good Friday morning from Caiaphas' palace to the Roman Governor's house. And they themselves would not enter the Judgment-hall, would not set foot on heathen ground, lest they should unwittingly contract defilement and so be unfitted to partake of the Paschal feast.[1] "Afraid of leaven, not afraid of innocent blood!"

Are there not parallel hypocrisies, self-deceits, to which we are exposed?

Can you imagine a person punctilious about matters of outward observance, while careless of true inward reverence, who would not think, for instance, of breaking the fast before Communion, yet not hesitating to receive the Sacrament after an outburst of temper, or with uncharitable or other evil thoughts allowed in the heart? You will not misunder-

---

[1] S. John xviii. 28.

HYPOCRISY.

stand me. Fasting Communion is a good and pious practice—a natural instinct of reverence, it would seem to me; more than that, it is the traditional custom of the Church from the earliest times, until low views of the Sacrament gained ground. The custom has a claim upon our observance wherever and whenever it is possible.[1] Outward and bodily reverence is not to be despised, nor faithfulness in little things. "These ought ye to have done," said our Lord, referring to the really important matters, "and not to leave the other undone." The whole of our religion is sacramental. It must be so, if it follow the law of the Incarnation, if it be true to the constitution of man's nature. Throughout it has outward and visible signs of inward and spiritual realities. But it is the inward reality which gives meaning and virtue to the outward sign. What are the bread and wine unless they be in truth the means whereby we receive the Body and Blood of our Lord? And of what value are outward observances save as guarding inner realities, or as the expression of the soul's devotion? Do let us take heed that we put not what is unessential and outward in the place of what is essential. Let us observe a due

---

[1] See a tract on *Fasting Communion* by the author, No. 8 of "Papers by Mission Priests of S. John the Evangelist."

proportion and subordination in all things. Too often, like the Pharisees, we strain out a gnat while we swallow a camel.

See an instance of quite a different kind. There are persons who would not take a pin from a neighbor, who yet systematically rob the poor on a large scale by disregard of such laws of Fair Wages as I referred to last Sunday, or by extravagant luxury and vain expenses.

3. There is, my brethren, need for us all to be on our guard, lest being occupied about religious things we should think ourselves necessarily religious. We must not think that the practice of religious observances will answer the same purpose as being really religious. Is there not room for the warning in Lent? The Services and Sacraments of the Church are intended to quicken within us the Spirit of Christ. Unless they do this, our participation in them is a kind of stage play. "If any have not the Spirit of Christ, he is none of His."[1] Otherwise religious exercises may bring on us, as on the Pharisees, even "the greater condemnation."

Let us now turn back for a minute to two great similes used by our Lord in these Woes, and see their possible application to ourselves.

---
[1] Rom. viii. 9.

(*a.*) In the twenty-fifth and twenty-sixth verses He points to the hypocritical cleansing of the outside of the cup and the platter. The vessels are carefully cleansed, their surface within and without. But how about the contents? They had been gotten by extortion; they are used for excess. "Thou blind Pharisee," our Lord says, "cleanse first that which is within, that the outside may be clean also." Aye, let us learn that lesson, to begin from within and work outward.

(*b.*) Then, in the twenty-seventh and twenty-eighth verses our Saviour, pointing perhaps to some neighboring sepulchres shining in their new whiteness, compares the Scribes and Pharisees, hypocrites, to the graves carefully whitewashed in the spring of every year, that men might avoid them, lest by coming in contact with that which was connected with death they should incur ceremonial defilement. Ye are like to such whited sepulchres, He says, which indeed appear beautiful outward, but within are full of dead men's bones and of all uncleanness. And note here a point of irony which perhaps we are apt to miss. As the whitewashing of the sepulchres gave an appearance of cleanness, but was really a warning of concealed uncleanness, so outward scrupulousness and obtruded show of righteousness may be a sign of much that is wrong within. Real righteousness within would be attended by a humility which is incompatible with all obtrusiveness. A religion which is obtrusive is probably superficial, neither very true nor very deep. A religious zeal which expends itself in trifles—whether of doctrine, or ritual, or observance—has not room or strength left for the weightier matters of the law. We cannot but be reminded again, my brethren, by such considerations, of His all-seeing, all-penetrating gaze, Whose eyes are as a flame of fire, Who is a discerner of the thoughts and intents of the heart, Who says to each one, "I know thy works."[1] We will again take warning from the case of Sardis, which had a name to live but was dead before God, held in reputation by others but whose works were not found perfect before Him.[2] This surely is a thought for Passiontide, as we enter on the last two weeks, the most solemn part of Lent, concerning the importance and necessity of self-examination before our Easter Communion. Such examination we will make by the rule and standard of God's commandments, "not lightly and after the manner of dissemblers with God, but so that we may come holy and clean to such a heavenly Feast."[3]

---

[1] Rev. ii. 18, 23.   [2] Rev. iii. 1, 2.
[3] Warning before Holy Communion, in the Prayer Book.

"Try me, O God, and seek the ground of my heart; prove me, and examine my thoughts.

"Look well if there be any way of wickedness in me; and lead me in the way everlasting."[1]

"From all blindness of heart; from pride, vainglory, and hypocrisy, Good Lord, deliver us."

---

[1] Ps. cxxxix. 23, 24.

VI.

THE WOE ON THE TRAITOR.

"The Son of man goeth as it is written of him: but woe unto that man by whom the Son of man is betrayed! it had been good for that man if he had not been born."
—S. MATTHEW xxvi. 24.

WE have taken the Woes of the Gospel in their chronological order, as they were pronounced by our Lord in the course of His ministry. It is not fanciful to trace in them, as they thus stand, a sort of moral sequence, an ascending or a descending scale, reaching a climax or sinking to an abyss, in the Woe which fitly falls for our consideration as we enter the Holy Week, the Woe on the Traitor.

The Woe on Worldly Contentment and Ease stands first. Wealth and worldly goods are external impediments to the pursuit of true and solid blessedness. Worldly Popularity is a more subtle and fascinating danger. The Abuse of Religious Privileges is still more dangerous, because it is the perversion of what are designed as blessings. A still deeper guilt attaches to the Causing others to Stumble. Hypocrisy while persisted in blinds the heart, the actor comes to think his own the part he continually plays. Such Hypocrisy naturally leads to Treachery—even to betraying the Son of Man with a kiss. One might almost say that Judas had passed through those earlier stages, had failed to take warning by the other Woes, ere he arrived at this pitch of iniquity and incurred this most awful doom.

I. Some of you will remember how the great mediæval poet places at the very bottom of the Infernal Pit the Traitors. Deep down below the Seducers, below the Hypocrites—with Caiaphas, Annas, and the rest of the Council that condemned our Lord for their chief representatives,—finally the Pool of Wailing is reached by Dante and his guide. A basin of ice it is represented, as fast bound in frost as are the affections of the Traitors who are locked therein. These are ranked in four classes and stages, each with a punishment more dreadful, answering to their deeper guilt, as Betrayers of their Kindred, Betrayers of their Country, Betrayers of their Friends and Guests, and Betrayers of their Benefactors and Lords. At the very bottom of the abyss is seen the Hell-Emperor (he "who once all created beauty led,")[1]—his ingratitude past estimation, past imagination, all but infinite—a monster with triple-faced head, holding and crunching in his three mouths the three worst Traitors of all—Judas Iscariot, Brutus, and Cassius. Traitors these three against the Divine Head and Founder of the Church, and against the Divinely appointed head and founder of the Roman Empire; sinners alike against God and against Humanity, sharers in the Sin of Satan, their treachery—to which they were severally led by Avarice, by Pride, by Envy—being aggravated, as was his, by ingratitude toward their benefactors.

"Woe unto that man through whom the Son of Man is betrayed! Good were it for that man if he had not been born." The awful sentence of Infinite Justice, the affecting lamentation of Infinite Love, finds an echoing verdict in the human conscience.

II. Note the singularly awful character of this Woe. It is the declaration of the Incarnate Word, the sentence of the unerring Judge, the lament of Infinite Love—"Good were it for

---

[1] *Shadow of Dante*, 59-103. Plumptre's Dante, Vol. I., p. 175, note. Comp. Isa. xiv. 12; Ezek. xxviii. 15. The Fathers interpreted the prophecies concerning the king of Babylon and the prince of Tyre of Satan.

that man if he had not been born." Do not our Lord's words close and settle the question, rule out the fallacious suggestion, of Universal Restoration to which some fondly cling? Do they not imply the possibility of endless existence in endless loss, declare it as a fact in the case of one? If the soul of Judas is hereafter, at however inconceivably remote a future, and through whatever agonies of purification, to be restored to the light of His countenance "in Whose presence is the fulness of joy," how then could the words be true, "It were better for him if he had never been born"? Who counts the billows when the shore is won? Who would cast back a moment's regret at the all but interminable vista of cleansing agony through which he had passed at length into the light of the Beatific Vision, to an eternity of blissful life? No, concerning one at least we have been told by the Truth Himself that God's purpose in His creation has been frustrated, and that without hope of recovery. There is a possibility of endless loss—for there is a lost, a hopelessly, irretrievably lost and ruined soul, who has gone to "his own place,"[1] not the place for which God would have fitted him, for which he was predestined, but that which by a life of

---

[1] Acts i. 25.

constant, sustained deceit, in spite of the drawings of a more than human love, and at last by an act of unparalleled treachery and baseness he earned, appropriated, and made "his own."[1]

Now, mark you, the instance of Judas has both its dread warning and its consoling reassurance.

1. Judas was an extreme case. Granted. Most certainly. None but extreme cases are lost. God loses none whom He can save consistently with His respect for the free-will with which He has endowed us. This He could not force without destroying our moral being. He rejects none who have not first—aye, and wilfully and persistently—rejected Him. He does not easily let any go. "He has no pleasure in the death of the wicked, but that the wicked turn from his way and live."[2] "He deviseth means that His banished be not expelled from Him," whereby they may return.[3] But what if they will not turn? if repudiated Grace and thwarted Love have to cry, "Ye will not come to Me?"[4]

2. Judas was an extreme case; but it was not therefore of necessity a unique case. The

---

[1] Luckock, *Footprints of the Son of Man*, Vol. II., p. 189.   [2] Ezek. xviii. 23.
[3] 2 Sam. xiv. 14.   [4] S. John v. 40.

falling away, and that hopelessly, of one so near to Jesus, who had been so highly favored, for whom his Master had such a different purpose, holds forth to us a dread warning as to such a possibility of utter reprobation for ourselves likewise.

Judas is surely a representative character. The Incarnation and the Passion (let me remind you) are a dramatic representation of the continual attitude of God towards the World and of the world towards God. They manifest the abiding relations between God and a fallen World. The life, the actions and sufferings of our Lord, the Word made flesh, unveil and make clear to the eye of sense what else belonged wholly to the spiritual sphere. In outward manifestation the mysteries were once accomplished. But the outward and literal accomplishment was the exhibition, as I said, in dramatic representation of what is continually being enacted in every age and in every land, aye, and in our individual lives. We read the story in our Bible. And a great part of its fascination for us lies in this, that we recognize in the Bible story that which we have witnessed in our own experience. Peter and Judas, Herod, Caiphas, and Pilate, and the rest, they are familiar figures, prominent in the drama which is ever being enacted on the stage of human life. The unjust, unprincipled judge, the jeering sensualist, the envious, crafty politician, the fickle crowd, the cowardly disciple, full of promises but failing at the point, the treacherous friend—we know them all. It is the Son of Man who suffers. It is this which gives meaning to the annual commemoration of our Lord's Passion. We are not merely recalling what happened once near a thousand years ago. The story is never old. We see ourselves.

> "My weak self-love and guilty pride
> His Pilate and His Judas were."

There is another aspect of the Passion as the climax of the age-long conflict between good and evil, right and wrong, love and hate, on which viewed in this light we should dwell. It is suggested, or hinted at, in the title by which our Lord designates Himself, "the Son of Man." In His Passion as throughout His life Jesus our Lord is Son of God and Son of Man. It is the Incarnate Word who is thus rejected. But this His enemies knew not. Had they known it, they would not have crucified the Lord of glory.[1] Their eyes were holden. But Judas knew that he betrayed the innocent blood,[2] that he was false to his Master, One whose character he knew as kind

---

[1] 1 Cor. ii. 8.   [2] S. Matt. xxvii. 4.

and true and good. To betray Him he sold himself for thirty pieces of silver.

So with us. We think it almost impossible for us to play the part of Judas. Only by a forced and strained application of the story can we place ourselves in his position and find ourselves guilty of his sin. In a way, indeed, we can turn on God present with us by His grace and truth. We can be false to our faith, to our conscience, can hand over sacred treasures, the honor of God and His Church to their enemies.

But false to our brother man we are perhaps more often tempted to be, and thus to play the part of Judas. We prove faithless to our friend, betray the innocent blood. We may betray any good cause knowingly, through avarice, pride, or envy, to gratify our spite, our self-love, in one form or another. So we share the guilt of Judas betraying the Representative Man who gathers up into Himself all good causes.

Crime may be committed against God in man, not only against God personally. Christ suffers in His members, Christ suffers as the representative of all men. It matters not whether it be the goodness of God in Himself or the goodness of God the Incarnate Son, or the goodness of God in any of His children. It is the same Goodness to which we are true or false. Truth, Goodness, Right are betrayed, denied, insulted; and thus is Judas' sin reproduced.

III. But it was not simply the fact of betraying the Son of Man that made Judas' case so hopeless. It was the condition of heart which led to this possibility. Sins are not measured by their external effect but by the will out of which they proceed. The sin against the Holy Ghost is no one act, however grievous, but wilful, persistent resistance to the Holy Ghost and His pleadings which would lead the sinner to repentance. The pious instinct of the Church has been to think that almost all who took part in the actual crucifixion of our Lord were won to believe in Him. Believing they drank the Blood which in unbelief they shed, S. Augustine says of the soldiers. "Father, forgive them, for they know not what they do," Jesus prayed.[1] Judas knew what he did. He was steeling his heart against what was right. This was his special sinfulness, that he acted against such light. He was wasting and turning to evil the gifts of God. He stood in the presence of the true Light, and his soul chose darkness. Judas was not like Peter. Peter was presump-

---

[1] S. Luke xxiii. 34.

tuous, self-reliant, boastful; he succumbed to temptation, overborne with fear; but he was sound at the core; he could protest, "Lord, Thou knowest all things, Thou knowest that I love Thee."[1] But Judas was rotten and untrue. He deceived himself; he played tricks with his conscience, till it ceased to answer true. He became "a devil," as our Lord declared.[2] He was not, remember, always a devil. Along two lines we can trace his declension.

1. Chosen he had been out of the wider circle of disciples to be one of the twelve Apostles, chosen not according to any mere arbitrary selection, but because each had in our Lord's eyes a certain fitness for the position.[3] There must have been in Judas noble qualities to have been attracted by and to the new Teacher; he had cast in his lot with the Prophet of Nazareth, had made sacrifices for His sake. Peter's question would apply to him as to the rest of the Twelve, "We have left all and followed Thee."[4] He was not, I say, always a devil. Nor did he become a devil all at once, by a single fall. It is the steps by which he descended, lower and lower still, till at the last he reached this pitch of baseness, that give such solemn warning. Step by step he was

---

[1] S. John xxi. 17. [2] S. John vi. 70.
[3] S. Mark iii. 13-19. [4] S. Matt. xix. 27.

covetous and ambitious, a hypocrite, deceiving and being deceived, a slanderer of those who hindered his covetousness, a betrayer, a suicide. He had begun

"A harmless child, by gold as yet unbought." [1]

Some root of bitterness there was, an ambitious, covetous spirit. Perhaps this had in part and unconsciously influenced him in coming to Jesus. He had dreamed of an earthly Messianic kingdom. Avarice and greed had crept in and marred the purity of that soul. Jesus knew it along with the capacities for good when He called and chose him. He saw into what fruits those seeds of evil might unfold. He saw too how it might be overcome. It was His design to sanctify Judas. His teaching would be sufficient to counteract the evil tendencies of his disposition. But alas! our Lord's words were ever in his ear, never in his heart. Judas heard and did continually the contrary to what he heard. How must his heart have often smitten him, and how must he have steeled it!

It is so with us. We are called by Jesus. He knows our dispositions, and He provides remedies for all faults. But we can, like Judas, thwart His grace. One sin harbored and allowed, it does not matter what, can work

---

[1] *Lyra Innocentium*, "Judas's Infancy."

our ruin. The besetting sin of any might have the same effect as that of Judas, destroying the good qualities of nature, frustrating the work of grace. In his case the sin happened to be covetousness; but any sin will have the same effect, untruthfulness, impurity and self-indulgence, pride and vanity, or disobedience. Is there in us any such ruling passion, a rift in the lute that spoils the music? Lenten self-examination should show us our real state before God. We should ask not merely what we have done? but what we are? our attitude toward God? have I an honest and good heart?

You have some such besetting fault. You are conscious of it. Your struggle through life is to be against that sin. All depends on this. Either you must master that sin, or that sin will master you. Every deadly sin poisons life—faith, hope, love; the last drop of poison destroys life.

2. There is another side to Judas' declension. He allowed evil; and he resisted good. Think of our Lord's dealing with Judas, how He sought to win him to repentance, to draw out his love.

A year before He had warned him. "Have not I chosen you twelve? and one of you is a devil."[1] To Judas along with the others He

---

[1] S. John vi. 70.

had addressed many warnings against covetousness.[1] He had entrusted Judas with the common purse; by giving confidence He had sought to win it.[2] On the evening before Palm Sunday He had defended Mary from the attack of Judas, while not exposing his wicked design.[3] At the Supper while He gave him a private sign, showing His knowledge of the false disciple's guilt, He screens him from the rest. "They knew not for what Jesus spoke."[4] He knelt at Judas' feet as before Peter and the beloved disciple. In the Garden, before all was consummated, while there was yet time for Judas to repent, He lovingly remonstrated with him, "Friend, wherefore art thou come?"[5]

See the pattern of His dealing with a sinful soul. How has He thus dealt with us, borne with us in times of carelessness, been mindful of us while we were all unmindful of Him, not easily taking a refusal, placing Himself in our way. If in spite of these opportunities, pleadings, warnings, we persist, surely we are placing ourselves in Judas' place, we incur his woe. He had seen the beauty, the love, and the power of Jesus, and turning from this there was naught to win him back.

---

[1] *E.g.*, S. Luke xii. 15; S. Matt. vi. 24.
[2] S. John xiii. 29.   [3] S. John xii. 4–8.
[4] S. John xiii. 26–29.   [5] S. Matt. xxvi. 50.

Deceiving and deceived he went on, until at last he was given over. Judas went out, "and it was night," says S. John.[1] It was night without and tenfold night within. Oh, the darkness that now settled upon the soul of Judas, when he finally rejected the warning voice of Jesus! "He that doeth evil hateth the light, neither cometh to the light, lest his deeds should be reproved."[2] It was night, says S. Augustine, when he went out; and he that went out was Night. The Light of Truth had been quenched. The Holy Spirit's flame put out.

And then, in a moment of distracting frenzy, he closed by a suicidal hand that life of which the Lord said: It were good for him if it had not been begun.

"Whichever way he looked was Hell,
Himself was Hell."

O Thou Who art the Light of the world, and the Light of our individual consciences, grant that we may never turn from Thee; enlighten us, shew us ourselves in our misery; shew us Thyself in Thy grace and truth. From all hardness of heart and contempt of Thy word and commandment; from all resistance to Thy grace, Good Lord, deliver us."

---

[1] S. John xiii. 30.   [2] S. John iii. 20.

BY THE SAME AUTHOR.

Sermons and Tracts.

	Cts.
THE WORDS FROM AND TO THE CROSS, MEDITATIONS	60
GOSPEL WOES (Lent Lectures)	60
SELF DISCIPLINE, Lenten Addresses........ 25 and	60
MEDITATIONS ON THE LIFE OF S. JOHN THE EVANGELIST	25
THE SAINTLY LIFE, Notes for Meditation on the Epistle to the Philippians	25
CONCERNING CHRIST AND THE CHURCH, A Devotional Exposition of the Epistle to the Ephesians	60
MEDITATIONS ON THE CREED	50
" " LORD'S PRAYER	50
" " EXAMPLE OF THE PASSION	35
" " COLLECTS (1. Advent to Trinity)	60
" " " (2. Trinity Season and Saints' Days)	60
EXPOSITION OF THE GOSPEL CANTICLES	50
REASONABLE FAITH, Four Sermons on Fundamental Christian Doctrines	20
THE INSPIRATION OF HOLY SCRIPTURE	10
READING THE BIBLE	5
CATHOLIC not PROTESTANT nor ROMAN CATHOLIC	15
APOSTOLIC SUCCESSION	10
THE EUCHARISTIC SACRIFICE	10
CONFESSION	10
THE CHRISTIAN LAW CONCERNING MARRIAGE AND DIVORCE	10
PRAYERS FOR THE DEPARTED, 5c.; THE COMMUNION OF SAINTS, 5c.; CHRISTIAN FRIENDSHIP, 10c.; RETREATS, 5c.; FASTING COMMUNION, 5c.; HINTS FOR LENT, 5c.; FASTING, 5c.	

Mission House of S. John the Evangelist, 44 *Temple St., Boston, Mass.*

www.ingramcontent.com/pod-product-compliance
Lightning Source LLC
Chambersburg PA
CBHW032241080426
42735CB00008B/946